MW00622923

Let's Explore
HIRAGANA
&
KATAKANA
A Picture Tour of the Japanese Alphabet

はじめての
ひらがな・カタカナ

Bret Mayer ブレット・メイヤー

Jリサーチ出版

Preface はじめに

Greetings, fellow Japan enthusiasts! And thank you for picking up this book! Flip through the pages, and you'll learn about hiragana and katakana, two of the fundamental writing systems in Japanese. Just flipping straight through might make it difficult to remember everything, though—you should really stop and take time to examine each page! Those pages contain valuable information including:

• How to read and write each character
• Pronunciation tips
• Sample vocabulary with illustrations
• History of how each character formed
• "Wacky" phrases in Japanese and English using featured vocabulary

Hiragana and katakana are the first writing systems schoolchildren in Japan learn, and now the awesome power of elementary school level literacy is in your hands. If you're looking for a fun and comprehensive introduction to reading and writing in Japanese, this book is it! You've already touched it—you can't put it back on the shelf now!

Bret Mayer

Let's enjoy studying hiragana & katakana together!!

Bu　Sensei

2

日本が好きな皆さんこんにちは! この本を手にとっていただきありがとうございます! ページをめくるとひらがなとカタカナという、2種類の基本的な日本語について学ぶことができます。ただページをめくるだけではすべてを覚えることは難しいかもしれません。ページをめくる手をとめて、ゆっくり読んでみてください! それぞれのページには次のようなとっても大切な情報が含まれています。

・それぞれの文字の書き方、読み方
・発音のヒント
・日本の地名や文化などを含む単語とイラスト
・ひらがなのなりたち
・取り上げた単語を使ったちょっと変わったおもしろいフレーズ

ひらがなとカタカナは日本の子どもたちが最初に習う書き文字です。この1冊には、小学生レベルの驚くほどたくさんの語彙が詰まっています。
もしもあなたが楽しく包括的な日本語の読み書きの入門書を探しているのなら、本書がまさにそれです! もう既にあなたの手の中に! 棚にはもう戻せない!

ブレット・メイヤー

一緒に楽しくひらがなとカタカナのお勉強をしよう‼

ぶ 先生

What is hiragana & katakana?
ひらがな・カタカナってなんだろう？

There are three different kinds of characters in the Japanese language; hiragana, katakana and kanji.

日本語には、3種類の文字があるよ。それぞれひらがな、カタカナ、漢字と呼ばれているんだ。

1. Kanji 漢字

Kanji was brought to Japan from China more than a thousand years ago. Initially, only the elite used kanji as written language. Later, katakana and hiragana was developed for common people to use. Both hiragana and katakana are simplifications of kanji.

漢字は1000年以上前に中国から日本に来たんだ。最初のころ、漢字はエリート層しか使わなかったんだけど、後にひらがなとカタカナが生まれて、多くの人に使われるようになったんだよ。ひらがなとカタカナは、漢字を簡単にしたものなんだ！

2. Hiragana　ひらがな

Nowadays, it is used to write native words when there are no kanji, kanji is too difficult for writer or reader, and kanji is too formal.

現在のひらがなは主に、漢字がない場合、漢字が書き手や読み手にとって難しすぎる場合、漢字が堅苦しい場合などに使われるよ。

3. Katakana　カタカナ

Katakana is used for writing foreign loanwords, representing onomatopoeia, scientific terms, and more!

カタカナは主に外来語、オノマトペ、理系の用語などを書くときに使われるよ。

This book focuses on hiragana & katakana!!
この本はひらがなとカタカナの本だよ!!

Contents　もくじ

Part 3　Onomatopoeia　オノマトペ

How to use this book
本書の使いかた
ほんしょ　つか

Interesting words to know including tourist spots and Japanese culture.
日本の地名や文化など、みんなが興味のある単語を集めたよ!
にほん　ちめい　ぶんか　きょうみ　たんご　あつ

Pronunciation tips!
発音の参考にしてね!
はつおん　さんこう

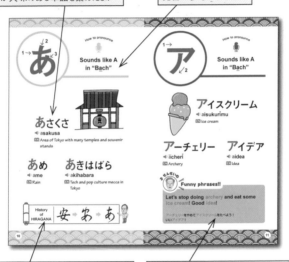

There are many opinions regarding the history of hiragana, so consider this a representative example.
ひらがなのなりたちは諸説あるけど、代表的なものを載せているよ!
しょせつ　だいひょうてき　の

Wacky phrases in Japanese and English using featured vocabulary.These are just silly phrases to show words in the context of a sentence. Don't take them too seriously.
取り上げた単語を使ったおもしろいフレーズだよ! ジョークだから、内容は信じちゃダメよ!
と　たんご　つか　ないよう　しん

Part 1

せいおん
清音

Basic characters

Sounds like A in "Bach"

あさくさ
🔊 **asakusa**

EN Area of Tokyo with many temples and souvenir stands

あめ
🔊 **ame**

EN Rain

あきはばら
🔊 **akihabara**

EN Tech and pop culture mecca in Tokyo

History of HIRAGANA

安 ➡ あ ➡ あ

売上カード

書名・著者名	発行所名
はじめ Let's Exp Bret Mayer	

ISBN9

発行所名 Jリサーチ出版

著者 Bret Mayer

書名 はじめてのひらがな・カタカナ
Let's Explore HIRAGANA & KATAKANA

定価 本体1000円+税

補充 注文 カ

貴店名(帖合)

注文数

ISBN978-4-86392-394-2
C0081 ¥1000E

9784863923942

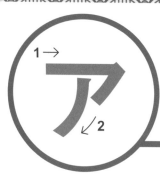

How to pronounce

Sounds like A in "Bach"

アイスクリーム
🔊 aisukurīmu

EN Ice cream

アーチェリー
🔊 ācherī

EN Archery

アイデア
🔊 aidea

EN Idea

Funny phrases!!

Let's stop doing archery and eat some ice cream! Good idea!

アーチェリーをやめてアイスクリームをたべよう！
いいアイデア！

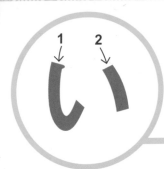

**Sounds like EE
in "eep!"**

いけばな
🔊 **ikebana**
EN Japanese flower arrangement

いぬ
🔊 **inu**
EN Dog

いえ
🔊 **ie**
EN House

History of HIRAGANA	以 ➡ い➡ い

Sounds like EE in "eep!"

イカ
🔊 ika
EN Squid

イクラ
🔊 ikura
EN Salmon roe

イチゴ
🔊 ichigo
EN Strawberry

Funny phrases!!

I'd like my strawberry smoothie with salmon roe and squid, please.

イチゴスムージーに、イクラとイカをいれてください。

13

**Sounds like U
in "uber"**

うどん
🔊 udon
EN Thick noodles made of wheat flour

うみ
🔊 umi
EN Ocean
Sea

うさぎ
🔊 usagi
EN Rabbit

History
of
HIRAGANA　宇 ➡ 宇 ➡ う

14

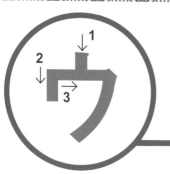

How to pronounce

**Sounds like U
in "uber"**

ウナギ

🔊 unagi

EN Eel

ウーパールーパー

🔊 ūpārūpā

EN Axolotl

ウルトラマン

🔊 urutoraman

EN Ultraman

Funny phrases!!

Let's go see "Ultraman VS the Axolotl"
then get some eel on the way home!

『ウルトラマンVSウーパールーパー』をみにいって、
ウナギをたべてかえろう！

えがお
🔊 egao
EN Smile

えき
🔊 eki
EN Train station

えんぴつ
🔊 enpitsu
EN Pencil

History of HIRAGANA 衣 ➡ え ➡ え

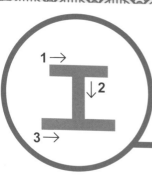

How to pronounce

Sounds like E in "pen"

エプロン

🔊 **epuron**

🇬🇧 Apron

エープリルフール

🔊 **ēpurirufūru**

🇬🇧 April Fool's!

エジプト

🔊 **ejiputo**

🇬🇧 Egypt

Funny phrases!!

I sent your favorite apron to Egypt. April Fool's!

あなたのおきにいりのエプロンをエジプトにおくった。
まさにきょうはエープリルフール！

17

Sounds like O
in "boat"

おんせん
🔊 **onsen**

EN Hot springs

おこのみやき
🔊 **okonomiyaki**

EN Assorted vegetables
cooked in batter

おきなわ
🔊 **okinawa**

EN Southernmost island
prefecture

 | History of HIRAGANA | 於 ➡ 〵 ➡ お |

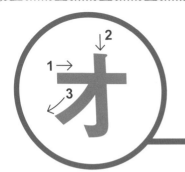

Sounds like O in "boat"

オートバイ

◀€ ōtobai

EN Motorbike

オークション

◀€ ōkushon

EN Auction

オーストラリア

◀€ ōsutoraria

EN Australia

 Funny phrases!!

I ordered an Australian motorbike off an online auction site.

オークションサイトでオーストラリアのオートバイをちゅうもんした。

Sounds like CO in "cop"

かぶき
🔊 **kabuki**

EN Traditional Japanese theater

かるた
🔊 **karuta**

EN Traditional Japanese playing cards

からて
🔊 **karate**

EN Traditional Japanese martial art

History of HIRAGANA	加 ➡ か ➡ か

$1 \rightarrow$ $\downarrow 2$

カ

How to pronounce

**Sounds like CO
in "cop"**

カラオケ

🔊 **karaoke**

EN Singing along with voiceless music
track

カナダ

🔊 **kanada**

EN Canada

カーナビ

🔊 **kānabi**

EN Car navigation

Funny phrases!!

**Hey, are there any karaoke bars in
Canada? I dunno, let's check the car
navigation…**

ねぇ、カナダにカラオケはあるの？
さぁね、カーナビでしらべてみよう…

Sounds like KEE
in "keep"

きもの
🔊 kimono

EN Traditional Japanese dress

きいろ
🔊 kīro

EN Yellow

きんようび
🔊 kin'yōbi

EN Friday

History of HIRAGANA	幾 ➡ き ➡ き

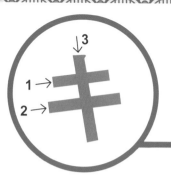

Sounds like KEE in "keep"

キジ
◀ kiji
EN Pheasant

キーボード
◀ kībōdo
EN Keyboard

キリン
◀ kirin
EN Giraffe

 Funny phrases!!

There's a pheasant and giraffe dancing on my keyboard. I can't get any work done!

キーボードのうえで、キジとキリンがおどっている。
ぜんぜんしごとができない！

23

Sounds like "coo"

くるま
 kuruma
EN Car

くも
 kumo
EN Clouds

くうこう
 kūkō
EN Airport

History
of
HIRAGANA | 久 ➡ く ➡ く

Sounds like "coo"

クッキー

🔊 kukkī

EN Cookie

クレジットカード

🔊 kurejittokādo

EN Credit card

クラッカー

🔊 kurakkā

EN Cracker

Funny phrases!!

I stole his credit card! Let's go buy tons of cookies and crackers!

かれのクレジットカードをぬすむんだ！クッキーとクラッカーを
たくさんかいにいこう！

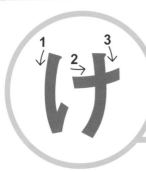

Sounds like KE in "Ken"

けんどう
🔊 **kendō**

🇬🇧 Japanese art of swordfighting

けんか
🔊 **kenka**

🇬🇧 Fight
Quarrel

けっこん
🔊 **kekkon**

🇬🇧 Marriage

| History of HIRAGANA | 計 → 計 → け |

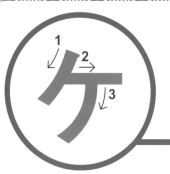

**Sounds like KE
in "Ken"**

ケーキ

🔊 kēki

EN Cake

ケチャップ

🔊 kechappu

EN Ketchup

ケニア

🔊 kenia

EN Kenya

 Funny phrases!!

**I heard that in Kenya they eat cake with
ketchup on it. Whaa? I don't believe it!**

ケニアではケーキにケチャップをつけてたべるってきいた。
またまたー！しんじないよ！

27

Sounds like CO in "cocoa"

こいのぼり
🔊 **koinobori**
🇬🇧 A carp-shaped wind sock

こめ
🔊 **kome**
🇬🇧 Rice

こま
🔊 **koma**
🇬🇧 Top

History of HIRAGANA | 己 ➡ こ ➡ こ

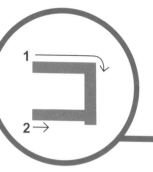

How to pronounce

Sounds like CO in "cocoa"

コーヒー
🔊 kōhī
EN Coffee

コート
🔊 kōto
EN Coat

コアラ
🔊 koara
EN Koala

Funny phrases!!

Hey! That koala just stole my coffee!
Quick, catch it with this coat!

あのコアラがぼくのコーヒーをぬすんだ！
はやくこのコートでつかまえろ！

29

さ

Sounds like SA in "Lisa"

さむらい
🔊 **samurai**

EN A Japanese warrior

さくら
🔊 **sakura**

EN Cherry blossom

さしみ
🔊 **sashimi**

EN Sliced raw fish

History of HIRAGANA	左 ➡ さ ➡ さ

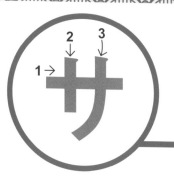

1→ 2↓ 3↓ **サ**

How to pronounce

Sounds like SA in "Li<u>sa</u>"

サイクリング
◀ **saikuringu**

EN Cycling

サッカー
◀ **sakkā**

EN Soccer

サイコロ
◀ **saikoro**

EN Dice

Funny phrases!!

Alright, roll the dice. If it's an odd number, let's play soccer. If it's an even number, let's go cycling.

さぁ、サイコロをふってみて。きすうなら、サッカーをしよう。
ぐうすうなら、サイクリングをしよう。

し

**Sounds like SHY
in "pu_shy_"**

しんかんせん
🔊 **shinkansen**
EN Bullet train

していせき
🔊 **shitēseki**
EN Reserved seat

しずおか
🔊 **shizuoka**
EN Shizuoka Prefecture

History of HIRAGANA	え ➡ 𛀁 ➡ し

Sounds like SHY in "pushy"

シーサー

🔊 shīsā

EN Okinawan lion-dog deity

シークワーサー

🔊 shīkuwāsā

EN Shequasar
Citrus fruit native to
Okinawa

シーザーサラダ

🔊 shīzāsarada

EN Caesar salad

せんせいの **Funny phrases!!**

Please pour shequasar from the mouth of that angry-looking Okinawan lion dog onto my caesar salad.

まじめなかおをしているシーサーのくちからシークワーサーを
ぼくのシーザーサラダにそそいでください。

33

Sounds like "Sue"

すきやき
🔊 sukiyaki
EN Beef and vegetable stirfry

すすき
🔊 susuki
EN Japanese pampas grass

すめし
🔊 sumeshi
EN Vinegared rice

History of HIRAGANA	寸 → 才 → す

How to pronounce

ス

1 →
2 ↘

Sounds like "Sue"

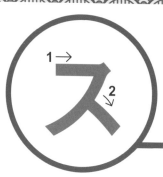

スープ
🔊 sūpu
EN Soup

スーツケース
🔊 sūtsukēsu
EN Suitcase

スケート
🔊 sukēto
EN Skating

Funny phrases!!

The thief sneakily pours soup into his suitcase and flees on skates.

スープをこっそりとスーツケースにそそぎ、スケートでにげるどろぼう。

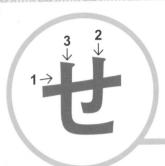

How to pronounce

Sounds like SE in "Seth"

せんす

🔊 sensu

🇬🇧 Folding fan

せんたくき

🔊 sentakuki

🇬🇧 Washing machine

せんべい

🔊 senbē

🇬🇧 Rice cracker

History of HIRAGANA	世 ➡ せ ➡ せ

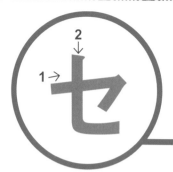

How to pronounce

Sounds like SE in "Seth"

セーラーふく
🔊 sērāfuku

EN Sailor uniform
Common school uniform

セミ
🔊 semi

EN Cicada

セルフサービス
🔊 serufusābisu

EN Self-service

せんせいの **Funny phrases!!**

Eating self-service shaved ice in a sailor uniform awash in the chirping of cicadas is the pinnacle of summer.

セミのなきごえをあびながら、セーラーふくでセルフサービスのかきごおりをたべるというのは、なつのだいごみです。

1 →
そ

Sounds like "sew"

そば
🔊 **soba**
🇬🇧 Buckwheat noodles

そうめん
🔊 **sōmen**
🇬🇧 Fine white noodles

そうじき
🔊 **sōjiki**
🇬🇧 Vacuum cleaner

History of HIRAGANA	曽 → そ → そ

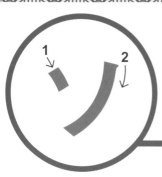

How to pronounce

Sounds like "<u>sew</u>"

ソース

🔊 sōsu

EN Sauce

ソーシャルメディア

🔊 sōsharumedia

EN Social media

ソーダ

🔊 sōda

EN Soda

せんせいの Funny phrases!!

I posted my sauce and soda latte to social media.

ソースとソーダいりのラテのしゃしんをとってソーシャルメディアにとうこうした。

た

Sounds like TO in "top"

たなばた
🔊 **tanabata**
EN The Star Festival

たこやき
🔊 **takoyaki**
EN Octopus baked into balls of batter

たたみ
🔊 **tatami**
EN Japanese straw floor coverings

History of HIRAGANA	太 ➡ た ➡ た

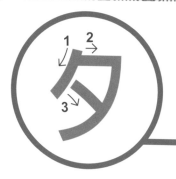

How to pronounce

Sounds like TO in "top"

タコ
🔊 tako
EN Octopus

タンバリン
🔊 tanbarin
EN Tambourine

タクシー
🔊 takushī
EN Taxi

せんせいの **Funny phrases!!**

Ah, we can't take this taxi. There's a tambourine-playing octopus riding it.

あぁこのタクシーはダメだ。タンバリンをたたくタコがのっている。

**Sounds like CHEA
in "cheap"**

ちよがみ
🔊 chiyogami
🇬🇧 Colorful origami folding
paper

ちかてつ
🔊 chikatetsu
🇬🇧 Subway

ちきゅう
🔊 chikyū
🇬🇧 Earth

History
of
HIRAGANA
知 → ち → ち

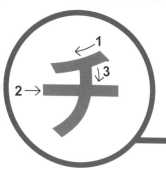

**Sounds like CHEA
in "cheap"**

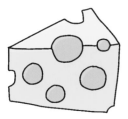

チーズ
🔊 chīzu
EN Cheese

チキンサンド
🔊 chikinsando
EN Chicken sandwich

チケット
🔊 chiketto
EN Ticket

 Funny phrases!!

I won a ticket for one free cheese &
chicken sandwich thumb-wrestling.

ゆびずもうでチーズ・チキンサンドのむりょうチケットをかちとった。

43

つ

1 →

How to pronounce

Try saying "What's oozing from your nose?" つ sounds like where "<u>T'S OO</u>" runs together.

つきじ
🔊 **tsu**kiji

🇪🇳 Area of famous fish markets in Tokyo

つき
🔊 **tsu**ki

🇪🇳 Moon

つけもの
🔊 **tsu**kemono

🇪🇳 Japanese pickles

 History of HIRAGANA 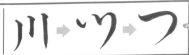 川 ➡ 'ワ ➡ つ

ツーショット
🔊 tsūshotto

EN Photo of two people together

ツナ
🔊 tsuna

EN Tuna

ツキノワグマ
🔊 tsukinowaguma

EN Black bear

Funny phrases!!

I lured out a black bear with some tuna and got this amazing shot of the two of us!

ツナでおびきよせてツキノワグマとこんなすばらしいツーショットがとれた！

Sounds like TE in "ten"

てんぷら
🔊 **tenpura**

🇬🇧 Tempura
Food served deep-fried

てんき
🔊 **tenki**

🇬🇧 Weather

ていしょく
🔊 **tēshoku**

🇬🇧 Meal set

History of HIRAGANA	天 ➡ て ➡ て

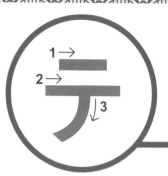

Sounds like TE in "ten"

テレビ

🔊 **te**rebi

EN Television

テニス

🔊 **te**nisu

EN Tennis

テーマソング

🔊 **tē**masongu

EN Theme song

Funny phrases!!

Before I play tennis, I like to watch Doraemon on television, and listen to its theme song. It gets me pumped!

テニスをやるまえに、ドラえもんのテレビをみて、テーマソングをきく。きあいがはいるぜ！

と

とうきょう
🔊 tōkyō
EN Capital of Japan

とんぼ
🔊 tonbo
EN Dragonfly

とうふ
🔊 tōfu
EN Soybean curd

 History of HIRAGANA 止 ➡ と ➡ と

トンカツ
🔊 tonkatsu

EN Fried pork

トマト
🔊 tomato

EN Tomato

トランプ
🔊 toranpu

EN Playing cards

 Funny phrases!!

Let's add a bet to our card game. If I win, I get your fried pork. If you win, I'll give you my tomato.

トランプでかけをしよう。わたしがかったら、きみのトンカツをもらう。
きみがかったら、わたしのトマトをあげる。

Sounds like NO
in "<u>no</u>t"

なっとう
🔊 nattō

EN Fermented soy beans

なす
🔊 nasu

EN Eggplant

なつ
🔊 natsu

EN Summer

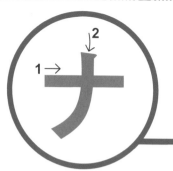

Sounds like NO in "<u>no</u>t"

ナース
🔊 nāsu
EN Nurse

ナッツ
🔊 nattsu
EN Nuts

ナップザック
🔊 nappuzakku
EN Knapsack

Funny phrases!!

Oh no! He is allergic to nuts! Hurry and call the nurse! Her phone number is in the knapsack!

やばい！かれはナッツアレルギー！はやくナースをよべ！
でんわばんごうはナップザックのなかにある！

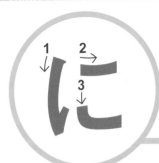

**Sounds like NI
in "u_ni_que"**

にんじゃ

🔊 **ninja**

EN Ninja
Professional spy in ancient Japan

にほんざる

🔊 **nihonzaru**

EN Japanese monkey

にちようび

🔊 **nichiyōbi**

EN Sunday

History of HIRAGANA	仁 ➡ 仁 ➡ に

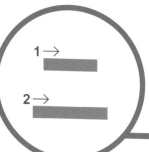

1 →

2 →

Sounds like NI in "unique"

ニット
🔊 nitto
EN Knit sweater or cap

ニッケル
🔊 nikkeru
EN Nickel

ニート
🔊 nīto
EN NEET
Not in Employment,
Education or Training

先せんせいの Funny phrases!!

You're a NEET, so I'm going to put you to work. You're going to knit sweaters. I'll give you a nickel for each one.

ニートのきみにいいしごとをあげよう。ニットをあむのだ。
いっちゃくにつき、ニッケルをひとつあげよう。

53

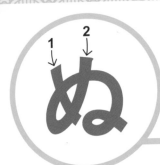

Sounds like "new"

ぬいぐるみ
🔊 **nu**igurumi
EN Stuffed animal

ぬえ
🔊 **nue**
EN Chimera

ぬりえ
🔊 **nu**rie
EN Coloring

History of HIRAGANA	奴 ➡ ぬ ➡ ぬ

Sounds like "<u>new</u>"

ヌンチャク

🔊 **nunchaku**

EN Traditional Okinawan martial arts weapon consisting of two fighting sticks tied together

ヌードル

🔊 **nūdoru**

EN Noodle

ヌガー

🔊 **nugā**

EN Nougat

Funny phrases!!

How dare you put nougat in my noodles! Prepare yourself! I'm going to bludgeon you with these nunchaku!

よくもわたしのヌードルにヌガーを！かくごしろ！
ヌンチャクでボコボコにしてやる！

How to pronounce

Sounds like NE in "net"

ねんがじょう
🔊 nengajō
EN New Year's cards

ねずみ
🔊 nezumi
EN Mouse

ねこ
🔊 neko
EN Cat

History of HIRAGANA | 祢 ➡ 祢 ➡ ね

Sounds like NE in "net"

ネットカフェ
🔊 **nettokafe**
EN Internet café

ネクタイ
🔊 **nekutai**
EN Necktie

ネイビー
🔊 **neibī**
EN Navy

Funny phrases!!

I went to an internet café wearing a fashionable navy necktie.

おしゃれなネイビーのネクタイをして、ネットカフェにいった。

Sounds like NO in "note"

のりまき

🔊 no**rimaki**

🇬🇧 Sushi wrapped in seaweed

のれん
🔊 no**ren**

🇬🇧 Hanging curtain at shop entrance

のはら
🔊 no**hara**

🇬🇧 Field

History of HIRAGANA	乃 ➜ 乃 ➜ の

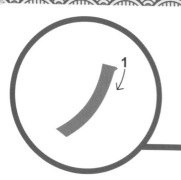

Sounds like NO in "<u>no</u>te"

ノートパソコン

🔊 **nōtopasokon**

🇬🇧 Abbrv. of notebook personal computer
Laptop

ノルウェー

🔊 **noruwē**

🇬🇧 Norway

ノート

🔊 **nōto**

🇬🇧 Notebook

Funny phrases!!

I put Norway flag stickers on my notebook and laptop.

ノートとノートパソコンにノルウェーのこっきのシールをつけた。

59

は

How to pronounce 🎤

Sounds like HO in "hot"

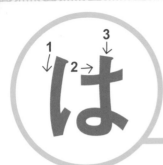

はねつき
🔊 **hanetsuki**

EN Japanese traditional game, similar to badminton

はな
🔊 **hana**

EN Flower

はし
🔊 **hashi**

EN Chopsticks

History of HIRAGANA	波 → 沈 → は

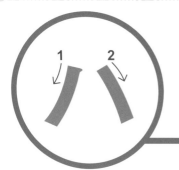

**Sounds like HO
in "hot"**

ハイタッチ
🔊 haitacchi
🇬🇧 High five

ハンバーガー
🔊 hanbāgā
🇬🇧 Hamburger

ハロウィーン
🔊 harowīn
🇬🇧 Halloween

Funny phrases!!

OK, for our Halloween costumes, I'll be a hamburger, and you'll be Hello Kitty. It's decided! High five!
では、ハロウィーンのコスチュームですが、わたしはハンバーガーにするからきみはハローキティね。きまった！ハイタッチ！

ひ

1 →

How to pronounce

Sounds like HEA in "heap"

ひろしま

🔊 **hiroshima**

EN Site of Hiroshima Peace Memorial Park

ひこうき

🔊 **hikōki**

EN Airplane

ひだり

🔊 **hidari**

EN Left

| History of HIRAGANA | 比 → 比 → ひ |

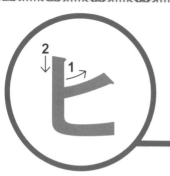

How to pronounce

Sounds like HEA in "heap"

ヒーロー

🔈 hirō

EN Hero

ヒップホップ

🔈 hippuhoppu

EN Hip hop

ヒキガエル

🔈 hikigaeru

EN Toad

Funny phrases!!

He's a hip hop star! His new album "Hero Toads" is a big hit!

かれはヒップホップのスター！あたらしいアルバム
『ヒーローのヒキガエル』がだいヒット！

Sounds like "<u>who</u>"

ふうりん
🔊 **fū**rin

🇬🇧 Wind chime

ふじさん
🔊 **fuji**san

🇬🇧 Mt. Fuji, the highest mountain in Japan(3,776.24 m)

ふゆ
🔊 **fuyu**

🇬🇧 Winter

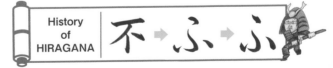

History of HIRAGANA | 不 ➡ ふ ➡ ふ

1 →

フ

How to pronounce

Sounds like "who"

フードコート
🔊 **fūdokōto**

EN Food court

フランス
🔊 **furansu**

EN France

フリーダイヤル
🔊 **furīdaiyaru**

EN Toll-free number

 せんせいの **Funny phrases!!**

For more information on food courts in France, call toll-free: 0120-123-4567.

フランスのフードコートのくわしいじょうほうはフリーダイヤル
0120-123-4567 まで。

65

1↗ **へ**

Sound like HE in "help"

へちま
 hechima
EN Sponge gourd

へび
 hebi
EN Snake

へいたい
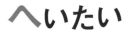 hētai
EN Troops

History of HIRAGANA  部 β ➡ ろ ➡ へ

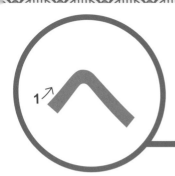

1 ↗

Sound like HE in "help"

ヘリコプター

🔊 **herikoputā**

EN Helicopter

ヘルメット

🔊 **herumetto**

EN Helmet

ヘッドフォン

🔊 **heddofon**

EN Headphone

Funny phrases!!

I want to ride in the helicopter, but I refuse to wear a helmet over my precious cat ear headphones!

ヘリコプターにのりたいけど、だいじなねこみみつきヘッドフォンの うえにはヘルメットをかぶらないよ！

Sounds like HO
in "hope"

ほっかいどう

🔊 ho**kk**aid**ō**

EN Hokkaidō prefecture
Northernmost prefecture in Japan

ほん

🔊 **hon**

EN Book

ほし

🔊 ho**shi**

EN Star

History of HIRAGANA	保 → 保 → ほ

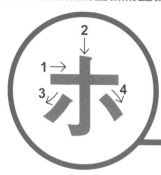

Sounds like HO in "hope"

ホタル
🔊 hotaru
EN Firefly

ホットケーキ
🔊 hottokēki
EN Pancake

ホテル
🔊 hoteru
EN Hotel

Funny phrases!!

If we go for a Premium Double at this hotel, they spread fireflies around the room, and we get free pancakes at breakfast.

ホテルをプレミアムダブルのへやにしたら、へやにホタルがはなたれ、ちょうしょくにむりょうでホットケーキがもらえます。

69

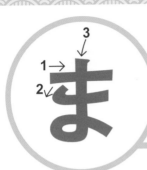

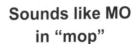

Sounds like MO in "mop"

まつり
🔊 matsuri
EN Festival

まんが
🔊 manga
EN Japanese comics

まんじゅう
🔊 manjū
EN Sweet bean paste with doughy shell

History of HIRAGANA | 末 → ま → ま

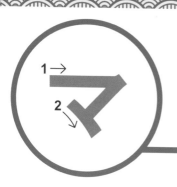

Sounds like MO in "mop"

マラソン
🔊 **ma**rason
EN Marathon

マネージャー
🔊 **ma**nējā
EN Manager

マネキン
🔊 **ma**nekin
EN Mannequin

 Funny phrases!!

Uncommon jobs: Manager for mannequin marathon

めずらしいバイト：マネキンのマラソンのマネージャー

み

Sounds like MI as in "do-re-mi"

みかづき
🔊 **mikazuki**

EN Crescent moon

みみ
🔊 **mimi**

EN Ear

みかん
🔊 **mikan**

EN Tangerine

History of HIRAGANA
美 ➡ 美 ➡ み

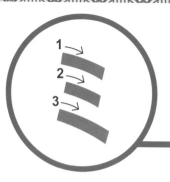

1 →
2 →
3 →

ミートソース

🔊 mītosōsu

EN Meat sauce

ミッドナイト

🔊 middonaito

EN Midnight

ミーティング

🔊 mītingu

EN Meeting

Funny phrases!!

We passionately debated meat sauce at a midnight meeting.

ミッドナイトのミーティングでミートソースについてあつくぎろんした。

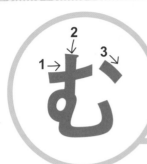

Sounds like MOO in "smooch"

むしめがね

🔊 **mushimegane**

EN Magnifying glass

むらさき

🔊 **murasaki**

EN Purple

むら

🔊 **mura**

EN Village

History of HIRAGANA | 武 → む → む

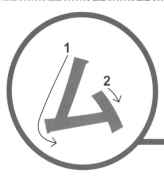

Sounds like MOO in "smooch"

ムース
◀ mūsu
EN Mousse

ムードメーカー
◀ mūdomēkā
EN Inspiring person

ムカデ
◀ mukade
EN Centipede

せんせいの Funny phrases!!

Sato is the inspiring person who gets the team in high spirits. He makes everyone laugh by spreading mousse on centipedes.

さとうせんしゅはほんとうにこのチームのムードメーカーだ。ムカデにムースをあびせてみんなをわらわせる。

75

Sounds like "meh"

めいじじんぐう
🔊 mējijingū

EN Meiji Shrine, built in Tokyo to enshrine Emperor Meiji

めがね
🔊 megane

EN Glasses

めいし
🔊 mēshi

EN Business card

History of HIRAGANA	女 ➡ め ➡ め

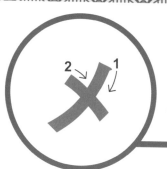

Sounds like "meh"

メイドカフェ

🔈 **mei**dokafe

EN Maid café
A themed café where staff dress
in maid outfits

メリークリスマス

🔈 **me**rikurisumasu

EN Merry Christmas

メール

🔈 **mē**ru

EN E-mail

Funny phrases!!

**Oh! I got a "Merry Christmas" e-mail
from my favorite maid café!**

おおー！すきなメイドカフェから「メリークリスマス」とかかれた
メールがきた！

**Sounds like MO
in "mope"**

もみじ
🔊 **mo**miji

🇬🇧 Japanese maple

もち
🔊 **mo**chi

🇬🇧 Pounded rice cake

もも
🔊 **mo**mo

🇬🇧 Peach

History of HIRAGANA	毛 ➜ 毛 ➜ も

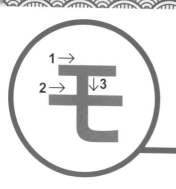

Sounds like MO in "mope"

モノレール
🔊 mo**norēru**
🇬🇧 Monorail

モッツァレラチーズ
🔊 mo**ttsarerachīzu**
🇬🇧 Mozzarella cheese

モンスター
🔊 mo**nsutā**
🇬🇧 Monster

Funny phrases!!

This monster appeared at the mall! I managed to run away by throwing mozzarella cheese at it and hopping on a monorail.

しょうてんがいのなかにモンスターがあらわれた！モッツァレラチーズをなげつけたら、モノレールにのってにげだした。

Sounds like YAH in "booyah!"

やきとり
🔊 yakitori
EN Grilled chicken

やきそば
🔊 yakisoba
EN Stir-fried noodles

やきにく
🔊 yakiniku
EN Grilled meat

| History of HIRAGANA | 也 → や → や |

Sounds like YAH in "boo<u>yah</u>!"

ヤンキー
🔊 yankī

EN Yankee, term for a delinquent

ヤギ
🔊 yagi

EN Goat

ヤッホー
🔊 yahhō

EN Yahoo!

せんせいの **Funny phrases!!**

Yahoo! I high-fived a juvenile delinquent riding a goat!

ヤッホー！ヤギにのっているヤンキーとハイタッチをきめた！

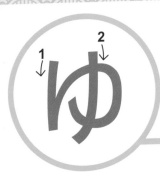

Sounds like YOO
in "yoo hoo!"

ゆかた
🔊 **yu**kata

EN Japanese summertime bathrobe

ゆき
🔊 **yu**ki

EN Snow

ゆめ
🔊 **yu**me

EN Dream

| History of HIRAGANA | 由 → ゆ → ゆ |

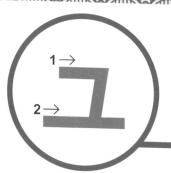

1→
2→

How to pronounce

**Sounds like YOO
in "yoo hoo!"**

ユーフォー
🔊 yūfō
🇬🇧 UFO

ユニーク
🔊 yunīku
🇬🇧 Unique

ユートピア
🔊 yūtopia
🇬🇧 Utopia

Funny phrases!!

**Last night, I had a unique dream. I got
abducted by a UFO and taken to a utopia
where dogs rule over humans.**

きのう、ユニークなゆめをみた。ユーフォーにゆうかいされて、
いぬがにんげんをしはいするユートピアにつれていかれた。

83

Sounds like "<u>yo</u>!"

ようかい
🔊 yōkai

EN Supernatural creature

ようかん
🔊 yōkan

EN Sweet bean jelly

よんコマ
🔊 yonkoma

EN 4-panel comic

| History of HIRAGANA | 与 ➡ ゟ ➡ よ |

84

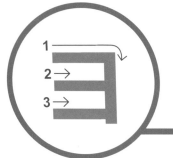

Sounds like "yo!"

ヨット
🔊 yotto
EN Yacht

ヨーグルト
🔊 yōguruto
EN Yoghurt

ヨーヨー
🔊 yōyō
EN Yo-yo

 Funny phrases!!

I'm taking a trip around the world on this yacht, so I'll prepare half a year's supply of yoghurt and a yo-yo to pass the time.

ヨットでせかいいっしゅうりょこうをするので、はんとしぶんの
ヨーグルトとひまつぶしのヨーヨーをよういする。

Sounds like a combination of
the LO in "lot" and
DO in "dot"

らくだ
🔊 **ra**kuda

EN Camel

らいしゅう
🔊 **raishū**

EN Next week

らく
🔊 **raku**

EN Easy
Relaxing

History of HIRAGANA	良 ➤ 良 ➤ ら

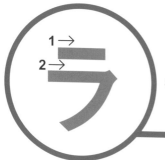

Sounds like a combination of
the LO in "lot" and
DO in "dot"

ラーメン
🔊 rāmen

EN Chinese noodles in soup

ランドセル
🔊 randoseru

EN Child's school backpack

ラムネ
🔊 ramune

EN Type of lemony soda

Funny phrases!!

I have a bunch of ramen noodles and
lemony soda in my backpack. Let's eat it
in the lounge.

ランドセルにラーメンとラムネがたくさんある。
ラウンジでしょくじをしよう。

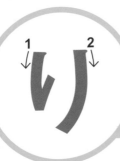

り
1↓ 2↓

Sounds like a combination of "Lee" and the letter "D"

りんご
🔊 **ringo**
EN Apple

りす
🔊 **risu**
EN Squirrel

りぼん
🔊 **ribon**
EN Ribbon

| History of HIRAGANA | 利 ➡ 利 ➡ り |

リ

How to pronounce

Sounds like a combination of "<u>Lee</u>" and the letter "<u>D</u>"

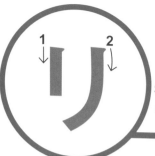

リフォーム
🔊 rifōmu
EN Home repair

リサイクルショップ
🔊 risaikurushoppu
EN Thrift store

リムジンバス
🔊 rimujinbasu
EN Airport shuttle bus

Funny phrases!!

I got this shuttle bus at the thrift store, so let's remodel the house and add a garage.

リサイクルショップでリムジンバスをかったため、いえをリフォームして、しゃこをつくろう。

Sounds like a combination of "Lou" and "dew"

るすばん
🔊 **rusuban**
🇬🇧 House-sitting

るり
🔊 **ruri**
🇬🇧 Lapis lazuli

るす
🔊 **rusu**
🇬🇧 Out of the house

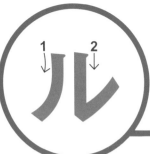

**Sounds like a combination
of "Lou" and "dew"**

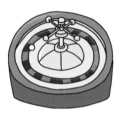

ルーレット

🔊 rūretto

EN Roulette

ルビー

🔊 rubī

EN Ruby

ルール

🔊 rūru

EN Rule

 Funny phrases!!

**When I play roulette, I always bet on
ruby red! It's my personal rule.**

ルーレットをやるとき、いつもルビーいろにかける。ぼくのルールさ。

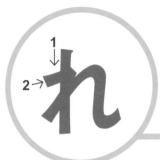

Sounds like a combination of "lay" and "day"

れんこん
🔊 renkon
EN Lotus root

れいぞうこ
🔊 rēzōko
EN Refrigerator

れんらく
🔊 renraku
EN Contact
Communication

| History of HIRAGANA | 礼 → 礼 → れ |

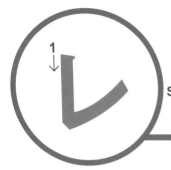

Sounds like a combination of "lay" and "day"

レンガ

🔊 renga

EN Brick

レモン

🔊 remon

EN Lemon

レース

🔊 rēsu

EN Race

 せんせいの **Funny phrases!!**

It's a race to the bricks over there!
Winner gets a lemon! Let's go!

あっちのレンガまでレースだ！しょうしゃにレモンを！レッツゴー！

93

1 → ろ

Sounds like a combination of "low" and "doe"

ろうそく

🔊 rōsoku
EN Candle

ろば
🔊 roba
EN Donkey

ろうか
🔊 rōka
EN Passageway

History of HIRAGANA	呂 ➡ ろ ➡ ろ

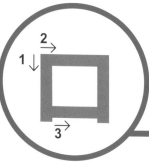

How to pronounce

Sounds like a combination of "<u>low</u>" and "<u>doe</u>"

ロボット
🔊 robotto
EN Robot

ロースト ビーフ
🔊 rōsutobīfu
EN Roast beef

ロケット
🔊 roketto
EN Rocket

せんせいの
Funny phrases!!

There's a robot that sells roast beef installed at the local convenience store.

ローストビーフをはんばいするロボットがきんじょのコンビニに
せっちされている。

Sounds like WHO
in "wh<u>o</u>pper"

わらびもち

🔊 **wa**rabimochi

EN Starch dumplings

わくせい
🔊 **wa**kusē

EN Planet

わがまま
🔊 **wa**gamama

EN Selfish

History of HIRAGANA	和 ➡ 和 ➡ わ

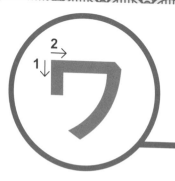

How to pronounce

**Sounds like WHO
in "whopper"**

ワニ
🔊 wani
EN Crocodile

ワッフル
🔊 waffuru
EN Waffle

ワンピース
🔊 wanpīsu
EN ONE PIECE, the title of a
popular Japanese comic

Funny phrases!!

**Luffy from "ONE PIECE" sent that
crocodile that ate my waffle flying!**

ぼくのワッフルをぬすみぐいしたワニを『ワンピース』のルフィが
ぶっとばしてくれた！

97

Pronounced same as お

すしをたべる

🔊 **sushiotaberu**

EN To eat sushi

えいがをみる

🔊 **eigaomiru**

EN To see a movie

やまみちをあるく

🔊 **yamamichioaruku**

EN To walk along a mountain path

History of HIRAGANA

遠 ➡ き ➡ を

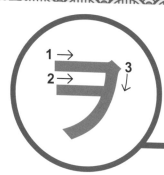

How to pronounce

Pronounced same as お

ヲタク

🔊 **otaku**

🇬🇧 Otaku, a term for a Japanese nerd heavily into anime, video games, comics or pop idols.

This is an exceptional case. This ヲ is used to stylize the word, and this is rarely used in Japanese writings.

ヲタク、この使い方は例外だよ。ここでは様式化するために使われていて、実際の日本語の書き文字では、ヲはめったに使われないんだ。

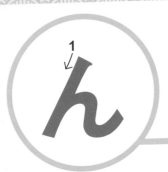

ふとん
🔊 futon

EN Japanese traditional style of bedding

しんぶん
🔊 shimbun

EN Newspaper

にんじん
🔊 ninjin

EN Carrot

History
of
HIRAGANA

| 无 ➡ ゑ ➡ ん |

パン
🔈 pan
EN Bread

インド
🔈 indo
EN India

ファン
🔈 fan
EN Fan

 How to pronounce

On the end of a word, sounds like the first N of a long, sarcastic "Nnnnnope." If followed by a B or P sound, becomes more like the first M of a delicious "Mmm mmm good!"

Let's write your name in katakana!! 1

なまえをカタカナでかいてみよう!! ①

Here is a sample of non-Japanese names written in katakana. Use these examples to help sound out and write your own name if it's not listed!

Alanna/Elena	アランナ・エレナ
Alexander/Alexandra/Alex	アレクサンダー・アレクサンドラ・アレックス
Amelia	アメリア
Andrew/Andy	アンドリュー・アンディー
Anthony/Tony	アントニー・トニー
Ariel	アリエル
Ashley	アシュリー
Barbara	バーバラ
Betty	ベティ
Brianna	ブリアンナ
Calvin	カルビン
Carol	キャロル
Charles/Chuck	チャールズ・チャック
Christopher/Chris	クリストファー・クリス
Daniel/Dan	ダニエル・ダン
David/Dave	デビッド・デーブ
Diana	ダイアナ
Diego	ディエゴ
Donald/Don	ドナルド・ドン
Dorothy	ドロシー
Elizabeth/Liz	エリザベス・リズ
Emily	エミリー
Emma	エマ
Fatima	ファティマ
Gabrielle/Gabby	ガブリエル・ギャビー
George/Jorge	ジョージ・ホルヘ
Hannah	ハナー
Hugo	ヒューゴ
Isabelle	イザベル
Ivan	イヴァン
James	ジェームズ
Jennifer/Jen	ジェニファー・ジェン

Part 2

だくおん はんだくおん
濁音・半濁音

Voiced consonants
&
Semi-voiced consonants

🎙️

Sounds like GO in "gotcha"

 すいぼくが

🔊 suiboku**ga**

🇪🇳 Ink wash painting

How to pronounce

🎙️

Sounds like GO in "gotcha"

ガールフレンド 🔊 **ga**rufurendo

🇪🇳 *Girlfriend*

ガソリン 🔊 **ga**sorin

🇪🇳 *Gasoline*

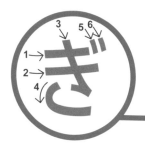

Sounds like GI in "give"

ぎんざ

🔊 gi**nza**

EN One of the most expensive shopping areas in Tokyo

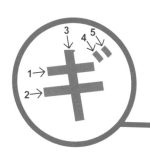

How to pronounce

Sounds like GI in "give"

ギター 🔊 gi**tā**
EN Guitar

ギックリごし 🔊 gi**kkurigoshi**
EN Trick back

Sounds like "<u>goo</u>"

てぬぐい

🔊 **tenugui**

EN Traditional Japanese hand towel

Sounds like "<u>goo</u>"

グレープフルーツ

🔊 **gurēpufurūtsu**

EN Grapefruit

グラス

🔊 **gurasu**

EN Glass, as in container for liquid

Sounds like GE in "get"

げいしゃ

🔊 **gei**sha

🇬🇧 A professional female entertainer performing several arts like Japanese traditional music and dance

How to pronounce

Sounds like GE in "get"

ゲームセンター 🔊 gēmusentā

🇬🇧 Video arcade

ゲームオーバー 🔊 gēmuōbā

🇬🇧 Game over

Sounds like "go"

ごま
🔊 goma

EN Sesame

Sounds like "go"

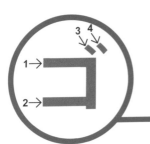

ゴール 🔊 gōru
EN Goal

ゴリラ 🔊 gorira
EN Gorilla

How to pronounce

Sounds like removing PIZ from "pizza" and just calling it "źa"

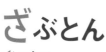

🔊 **za**buton

EN A floor cushion

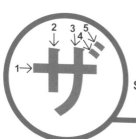

How to pronounce

Sounds like removing PIZ from "pizza" and just calling it "źa"

ザクロ 🔊 **za**kuro

EN Pomegranate

アザラシ 🔊 a**za**rashi

EN Seal

Sounds like the letter <u>G</u>

じんりきしゃ

🔊 jinrikisha

EN Rickshaw

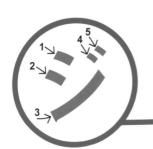

How to pronounce

Sounds like the letter <u>G</u>

ジーンズ 🔊 jīnzu
EN *Jeans*

ジム 🔊 jimu
EN *Gym*

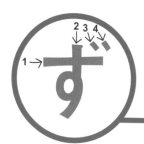

Sounds like "zoo"

いずもたいしゃ

🔊 **izu**motaisha

EN One of the most ancient Shinto shrines in Japan

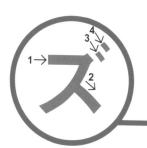

How to pronounce

Sounds like "zoo"

ズッキーニ 🔊 **zukkīni**
EN Zucchini

コンタクトレンズ 🔊 **kontakutoren**zu
EN Contact lens

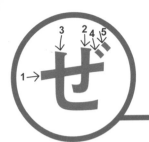

Sounds like ZE in "zen"

ざぜん

🔊 **zazen**

EN A typical meditative discipline in Zen Buddhism

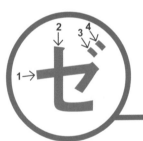

How to pronounce

Sounds like ZE in "zen"

ゼロ   🔊 **zero**
EN Zero

ゼラチン   🔊 **zerachin**
EN Gelatin

How to pronounce

Sounds like ZO in "Zoey"

しんぞう ◀ shinzō
EN The heart(organ)

ぞうきばやし ◀ zōkibayashi
EN Mixed-tree grove

How to pronounce

Sounds like ZO in "Zoey"

ゾンビ ◀ zonbi
EN Zombie

ゾロめ ◀ zorome
EN Snake eyes

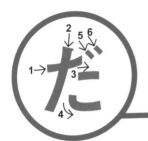

Sounds like DO in "dock"

だるま

🔊 **daruma**

EN Dharma doll

Sounds like DO in "dock"

ダーリン 🔊 dārin
EN Darling

ダウンロード 🔊 daunrōdo
EN Download

Sounds like DE in "den"

はつもうで

🔊 hatsum**ō**de

EN The first Shinto shrine visit of the Japanese New Year

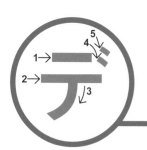

How to pronounce

Sounds like DE in "den"

デミグラスソース 🔊 **de**migurasus**ō**su

EN Demi-glace sauce

デート 🔊 d**ē**to

EN Date, as in a romantic date

Sounds like "D'oh!"

どうとんぼり

🔊 **dō**tonbori

EN One of the principal tourist destinations in Osaka, Japan

Sounds like "D'oh!"

ドア 🔊 **do**a

EN Door

ドイツご 🔊 **do**itsugo

EN German language

Nice to meet you. ➡ はじめまして　hajimemashite

Goodbye. ➡ さようなら　sayōnara

Good morning. ➡ おはよう　ohayō

Good afternoon. ➡ こんにちは　kon'nichiwa

Good evening. ➡ こんばんは　konbanwa

Good night. ➡ おやすみなさい　oyasuminasai

Thank you. ➡ ありがとう　arigatō

I'm sorry. ➡ ごめんなさい　gomen'nasai

Sounds like BO in "bop"

かまくら**ば**くふ

🔊 kamakura**ba**kufu

EN A Japanese feudal military government ruled from 1185 to 1333

How to pronounce

Sounds like BO in "bop"

バー 🔊 ba͞

EN Bar
Pub

バルーン 🔊 bar͞un

EN Balloon

How to pronounce

Sounds like BEE in "beep"

びわこ

◀ **biwako**

EN Lake Biwa, the largest lake in Japan

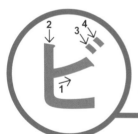

How to pronounce

Sounds like BEE in "beep"

ビリヤード ◀ **biriyādo**
EN Billiards

ビル ◀ **biru**
EN Building

🎤

Sounds like BOO in "boot"

びょうぶ

🔊 byōbu

EN Folding screen

How to pronounce

🎤

Sounds like BOO in "boot"

ブルーベリー　🔊 burūberī

EN Blueberry

ブーツ　🔊 būtsu

EN Boots

How to pronounce

Sounds like BE in "<u>bet</u>"

べんとう 🔊 ben**tō**
EN Boxed lunch

べったらづけ 🔊 **bettarazuke**
EN A kind of pickled daikon

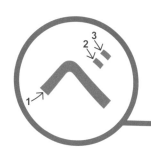

How to pronounce

Sounds like BE in "<u>bet</u>"

ベッド 🔊 be**ddo**
EN Bed

ベーコン 🔊 b**ē**kon
EN Bacon

How to pronounce

Sounds like BO in "boat"

うめぼし

🔊 **umeboshi**

EN Japanese salted plums

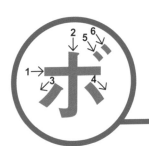

How to pronounce

Sounds like BO in "boat"

ボランティア 🔊 **borantia**

EN Volunteer

ボーナス 🔊 **bōnasu**

EN Bonus

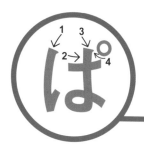

Sounds like PO in "pop"

かっぱ

🔊 kappa

EN Kappa, river-dwelling goblin

Sounds like PO in "pop"

パチンコ

🔊 pachinko

EN Popular game similar to Plinko

パーティー

🔊 patī

EN Party

Sounds like "pea"

はっぴ

🔊 **happi**

🇬🇧 Festival coat often decorated with town symbol

How to pronounce

Sounds like "pea"

ピザ 🔊 piza
🇬🇧 Pizza

ピアノ 🔊 piano
🇬🇧 Piano

Sounds like POO in "poop"

おんぷ 🔊 **onpu**
EN Musical notation

まんぷく 🔊 **manpuku**
EN Full stomach

How to pronounce

Sounds like POO in "poop"

プール 🔊 **pūru**
EN Pool

プリン 🔊 **purin**
EN Pudding

How to pronounce

Sounds like PE in "pep"

ほっ ぺ °　◀ hoppe
EN Cheek

かん ぺ °き　◀ kanpeki
EN Perfect

How to pronounce

Sounds like PE in "pep"

ペ °ンキ　◀ penki
EN Paint

ペ °ージ　◀ pēji
EN Page

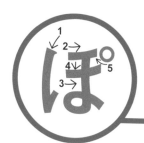

How to pronounce

Sounds like PO in "poke"

たんぽぽ 🔊 **tanpopo**
EN Dandelion

からっぽ 🔊 **karappo**
EN Empty

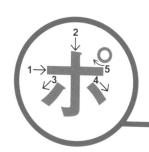

How to pronounce

Sounds like PO in "poke"

ポスト 🔊 **posuto**
EN Mailbox

ポエム 🔊 **poemu**
EN Poem

Let's take a break!! ①

As you progress through this book, diligently practicing each character and eagerly absorbing related vocabulary, you may be wondering what the box in the bottom left-hand corner is. This area shows the development of each hiragana character in three stages.

First, is the original kanji, or "Chinese character", from which the hiragana derived. Before the introduction of kanji, Japan did not have an official writing system. Kanji were first brought over to Japan from China in the first century AD, and began serious adoption after the fifth century AD.

The second, middle character, is a sample cursive form of the original kanji. This cursive script, known as 草書 [sousho], served as a somewhat messy shorthand. Nowadays, cursive script is a cherished art form in calligraphy and is used to produce beautiful brush work, but originally, it was utilized to record information quickly and efficiently. Imagine a hastily written doctor's prescription today being lauded as an example of traditional art several thousand years from now!

The third character shows the evolutionary step from cursive to hiragana. In modern-day Japan, hiragana complements kanji in Japanese writing. While Kanji depict images, ideas and concepts, hiragana represent syllables, or the sound of words.

For example, the kanji 歩 has a common meaning of "walk", but needs context to effectively convey information. Alone, it could be someone's name (歩 "Ayumi"); or after a number, it could be "ten thousand steps" 10000歩 [ichi man po] counted on a "pedometer" 万歩計 [manpokei]. Hiragana can indicate 歩 as part of the verb "to walk" 歩く [aruku] and even the verb tense, as in "I walked to the station" 駅まで歩いた [eki made aruita].

As you'll notice throughout the book, entire sentences can be written in hiragana with no need for kanji. Schoolchildren in Japan learn hiragana before katakana or kanji, and children's books are often written in full hiragana. Spacing after verb endings and particles helps the sentences read smoothly.

Take the sentence "I sent a cute cat photo to my best friend" 親友にかわいい猫の写真を送った。[shin'yuu ni kawaii neko no shashin o okutta]. In hiragana only, it may become しんゆうに　かわいいね

この　しゃしんを　おくった。

While you don't want to solely rely on hiragana forever, there's no need to panic about kanji right now if you're just starting your Japanese learning journey. Enjoy practicing hiragana and using it to communicate as much as you can!

ひらがなとカタカナを練習したり単語を覚えたりして、この本をこつこつ読み進めている皆さんの中には、Part 1 の左ページの下にある囲みはなんだろうと不思議に思った人もいるかな。この囲みは、ひらがなのなりたちを3段階で紹介しているんだ。

最初のは、ひらがなの由来になった、昔の漢字や「中国語の文字」。漢字が伝わる前、日本にはきちんとした文字がなかったんだ。西暦1世紀頃、中国から日本に漢字が伝わり、西暦5世紀以降、広く使われるようになったんだ。

真ん中のは、昔の漢字の筆記体の1例。草書と呼ばれるこの筆記体は、ちょっと乱雑な速記体だったんだ。今では書道の大切な芸術的字体の一つであり、美しい筆致を出すために用いられているけど、もともとは情報をより速く効率よく記録するのに使われていたんだ。医者が今日なぐり書きした処方箋が、これから数千年後に伝統的な芸術の一つとして称賛されているのを想像してみて！

3つめの文字は、草書からひらがなに進化したもの。現在、日本語の文章内で、ひらがなは漢字を補う役割をしている。漢字がイメージや概念、コンセプトを表す一方、ひらがなは音節を示したり、単語の音を表しているんだ。

例えば、漢字の「歩」の一般的な意味は「歩く」だけど、きちんと意味を伝えるには文脈が必要。1文字だけで人の名前（歩のよう）に使ったり、数字の後につけて「歩数計」（万歩計）で計った10000歩のように使うこともある。ひらがなと使うことで「歩」は「歩く」という動詞になったり、「駅まで歩いた」のように時制を示すことができるんだ。

この本を読んでいて気づいたとおり、文章全体を漢字を使わずにひらがなで書くことができる。日本の小学生はカタカナや漢字の前にひらがなを習うし、子供向けの本にはすべてひらがなで書かれたものもたくさんある。動詞、てにをはの後ろに空白を入れると、ひらがなだけの文章が読みやすくなるよ。
例えば、「親友にかわいい猫の写真を送った」。ひらがなだけで書くとこうなる、しんゆうにかわいいねこの　しゃしんを　おくった。

ずっとひらがなだけに頼りたくはないだろうけど、日本語学習の道に足を踏み入れたばかりなら、漢字への不安や恐れなんてまったく必要なし。ひらがな習得を楽しんで、たくさんのことをひらがなで伝えることを楽しもう！

Excuse me. ➡ すみません　sumimasen

Long time no see. ➡ ひさしぶり　hisashiburi

See you! ➡ またね！　matane

You're welcome.
➡ どういたしまして　dōitashimashite

Congratulations! ➡ おめでとう！　omedetō

I'm leaving. ➡ いってきます　ittekimasu

Have a safe trip.
➡ いってらっしゃい　itterasshai

Hi, I'm home. ➡ ただいま　tadaima

Welcome back. ➡ おかえり　okaeri

Japanese say "いただきます" (itadakimasu) before a meal and "ごちそうさま" (gochisō sama) after a meal.

Part 3

オノマトペ

Onomatopoeia

What is onomatopoeia?
オノマトペってなんだろう？

Onomatopoeias are used very often in Japanese, both in general conversations and written language. This is because they allow you to directly express what you see, feel, or think in your mind. They are also extremely useful because they help speakers or writers to describe sounds correctly and make stories more interesting.

Generally, onomatopoeia is categorized into following three types in Japanese:

- 擬音語 giongo : Onomatopoeia that is imitative of noises in nature or inanimate objects. (e.g. 雨がザーザー降る amegaザーザーfuru)

- 擬声語 gisēgo : Onomatopoeia that is imitative of humans and animals. (e.g. 犬がワンワン吠える inugaワンワンhoeru)

- 擬態語 gitaigo : Onomatopoeia that is description of states of being. (e.g. だらだらする daradarasuru)

オノマトペは、普段の会話でも書き言葉でもとても頻繁に使われているよ。それは、あなたが見たもの、感じたこと、考えていることなどを直接表現できるからだよ。また、オノマトペは、話し手や書き手が音を正確に表せるし、話をよりおもしろくしてくれるから、とても便利なんだ。

一般的に、オノマトペは日本語では次の3つに分けられているよ。

- **擬音語：** 自然界の音や物の音などを表す
- **擬声語：** 人間や動物の声を表す
- **擬態語：** 物事の様子や状態を表す

Let me introduce some common Japanese onomatopoeia.
Let's have a look at the next page!!

日常でよく使われるオノマトペを紹介するよ！さっそく
次のページにいってみよう!!

わらう -Laugh-

smile giggle
laugh smirk
grin chuckle

ゲラゲラわらう

🔊 **geragerawarau**

EN To guffaw
A loud, uncontrollable laugh

にこにこわらう

🔊 **nikonikowarau**

EN To smile
A nice bright smile

ヘラヘラわらう

🔊 **herahera**warau

EN To smirk
A dopey or foolish laugh

クスクスわらう

🔊 **kusukusu**warau

EN To giggle
A private giggle or chuckle

ニヤリとわらう

🔊 **niyarito**warau

EN To grin
A suggestive smile

おこる -Get angry-

fume anger
annoying irritating
furious

ぷんぷんおこる

🔊 punpun'**okoru**

EN To fume with anger

カンカンにおこる

🔊 kankan'**niokoru**

EN To grow furious

ムカつく

🔊 mukatsuku

EN Annoyed or irritated

カッとなる

🔊 kattonaru

EN To blow your top
To lose your cool

ムッとする

🔊 muttosuru

EN To be miffed
To stew quietly

なく -Cry-

sad cry weep upset tears

えーんえーん

🔊 ēn'ēn

EN A child crying

おぎゃあおぎゃあ

🔊 ogyāogyā

EN An infant crying

しくしくなく

🔊 shikushiku'**naku**

EN Weep
To cry softly

わんわんなく

🔊 wanwan'**naku**

EN To cry loudly

めそめそする

🔊 mesomeso**suru**

EN To shed tears
To cry softly

ねむる -Sleep-

drowsy
fast asleep   sleep
nod off   peaceful

ぐうぐう

🔊 gūgū

EN Fast asleep

とろんとする

🔊 toron**tosuru**

EN To be drowsy

ぐっすり**ねる**

🔊 **gussuri**neru

EN To sleep soundly
   To sleep tight

すやすや**ねる**

🔊 **suyasuya**neru

EN To sleep peacefully
   To sleep like an angel

うとうと**する**

🔊 **utouto**suru

EN To nod off

Let's take a break!! ②

We covered how hiragana evolved from kanji to cursive to the simplified characters used today, but what about katakana? The katakana alphabet is often associated with "foreign loanwords," but it's so much more!

If hiragana were created by "breaking down" an entire character into a simplified shape, katakana were created by "breaking apart" characters and using just a single component. For example, the katakana イ (Hiragana い) comes from the left side of 伊, which shares its pronunciation (sounds like the letter "E"). Katakana エ (Hiragana え) comes from the right side of 江, which also shares a pronunciation (sounds like "eh").

Sometimes katakana and hiragana are derived from the same character. Katakana カ is the left side of 加— it takes the piece as is and 口 is tossed in the bin. The hiragana か takes 加, smooths out the corners on カ and reduces 口 on the right to just a dot.

Katakana is often used for foreign loanwords. Most countries around the world are written in katakana, like America アメリカ, Australia オーストラリア, France フランス and India インド. Words adopted from other languages get the katakana treatment, too, like "personal computer" パソコン [pasokon] from English, "part-time job" アルバイト [arubaito] from German, "chou à la crème" シュークリーム [shu-kuri-mu] from French, or "ramen noodles" ラーメン [ra-men] from Chinese.

Now, if you spot katakana on signage, it doesn't automatically mean it's a foreign word! Another common usage is for emphasis, similar to italics or bold font. Also, people may opt for katakana over kanji for simplicity or project a certain atmosphere.

Consider "coffee," pronounced [ko-hi-], in Japanese: A small, privately run coffee shop aiming for a cozy, nostalgic vibe may adorn their signage with 珈琲, while a global chain of coffee shops goes with the katakana コーヒー for its modern look and feel along with simplicity of branding menus and merchandise.

These associations with emphasis and being modern and unique has lent katakana to only being used in "short bursts" and inappropriate for long text. Full sentences in katakana convey a strange, robotic feel and are often used for just that: speech coming from an alien or robot in a comic, cartoon, game, etc. One unfortunate side effect is foreigners that appear on television can end up subtitled in katakana to represent their awkward and stilted Japanese. If you ever end up ambushed in Tokyo for a "person on the street"-type interview, be sure to catch it when it airs. If they subtitle you with hiragana and kanji, you know you've made it as a student of Japanese!

ひらがながどうやって漢字から草書となり今日使われる簡素化された文字になっていったかは取り上げたけど、じゃあカタカナは？ カタカナの文字は「外来語」と関連付けられることが多いけど、本当にとっても多いんだ！

ひらがなが文字全体を簡素な形に「潰して」作られたとしたら、カタカナは文字を「分解して」1要素だけ使って作られた感じかな。例えば、カタカナの「イ」（ひらがなでは「い」）は「伊」の左側がもとになってて、発音（「E」のような音）も共にしているんだ。カタカナの「エ」（ひらがなでは「え」）は「江」の右側がもとになってて、こちらも発音（「eh」のような音）を共有している。

カタカナとひらがなが、同じ文字に由来していることもあるよ。カタカナの「カ」は「加」の左側だね──左側の要素そのままで「ロ」はゴミ箱にポイされちゃってる。ひらがなの「か」は「加」がもととなって、「カ」の角が滑らかになって、右側の「ロ」はただの点に単純化されているんだ。

カタカナは外来語によく使われるよ。世界中のほとんどの国はカタカナで書かれるよ、Americaならアメリカ、Australiaはオーストラリア、Franceはフランス、Indiaはインドみたいに。他言語の単語もカタカナの扱いを受けるよ、英語の「personal computer」ならパソコン、ドイツ語の「part-time job」（Arbeit「仕事」）由来のアルバイト、フランス語の「chou à la crème」はシュークリーム、中国語の「ramen noodles」（拉麺・拉面）由来のラーメンみたいに。

でもね、もし看板にカタカナを見つけたとしても、それが直ちに外国の単語というわけにはならないんだ！ ほかの一般的な使用法に、斜体や太字と似て、強調のために使われることもあるんだよ。さらに、シンプルさのために漢字ではなくカタカナを用いてもいいし、なんらかの雰囲気を伝えてもいいんだ。

日本語で［コーヒー］と発音する「coffee」について見てみよう。居心地のいいノスタルジックな雰囲気をねらった小さな個人経営の喫茶店なら店名を「珈琲」で飾るかもしれないし、一方世界的チェーンのコーヒーショップでは、ブランド化したメニューや商品のシンプルさと連動して、現代的な外観と雰囲気をだすためにカタカナの「コーヒー」を採用するんだ。

強調、現代的、そして独自性を連想させることは、カタカナが「一気」に使われるときのみで、長い文章にはそぐわないんだ。カタカナで全ての文を記すことは、奇妙でロボットのような感じを与え、そうしたいときにだけよく用いられる、例えばコミックやゲームなどのエイリアンやロボットのセリフだったり。残念な副作用として、テレビにでる外国人の下手で堅い日本語を表すのに、やっぱりカタカナのテロップがついてしまうこと。もし君が東京で待ち伏せしている「街角の人」インタビューを受けることになってしまったら、それが放送されるのを絶対見てみて。ひらがなと漢字のテロップだったら、日本語学習者として君は大成功しているよ！

おと ① -Sound 1-

flapping
knocking clanging
rattling pounding

ガタガタ

🔊 gatagata

EN Rattling sound

バタバタ

🔊 batabata

EN Flapping sound

トントン

🔊 tonton

EN Knocking

ドンドン

🔊 dondon

EN Pounding

ガンガン

🔊 gangan

EN Clanging

おと ② -Sound 2-

scream shock panting
squeak kissing
disgust

キャー!

🔊 kyā

EN Scream of shock or fright

ゲッ!

🔊 ge

EN Sound of disgust or dread

ゼーゼー

🔊 zēzē

EN Sound of panting

キュンと

🔊 kyun**to**

EN Sound of heart skipping a beat

チュッ

🔊 chu

EN Mouse squeaking
Kissing sound

いろいろなオノマトペ
A variety of onomatopoeia

flirting restless packed tight drenched messy

イチャイチャ

🔊 ichaicha

EN Flirting

キョロキョロ

🔊 kyorokyoro

EN Restlessly

びしょびしょ

🔈 bishobisho

EN Drenched

ごちゃごちゃ

🔈 gochagocha

EN Messy
Disorderly

ぎゅうぎゅう

🔈 gyūgyū

EN Packed tight
Squeezed in

Let's write your name in katakana!! 2
なまえをカタカナでかいてみよう!! ②

Here is a sample of non-Japanese names written in katakana. Use these examples to help sound out and write your own name if it's not listed!

Jonathon/John	ジョナサン・ジョン
Joseph/Joe	ジョセフ・ジョー
Karen	カレン
Katherine/Katie	キャサリン・ケイティ
Linda	リンダ
Lisa	リサ
Luke/Luca/Lucas	ルーク・ルーカ・ルーカス
Margaret	マーガレット
Maria	マリア
Mark/Marc	マーク
Mary	メアリー
Michael/Mike	マイケル・マイク
Mohamed	モハメッド
Nancy	ナンシー
Naomi	ナオミ・ネヨミ
Nathan	ネイサン
Nina	ニナ
Noel	ノエル
Olivia	オリビア
Patricia/Pat	パトリシア・パット
Paul	ポール
Richard/Rick	リチャード・リック
Robert/Bob	ロバート・ボブ
Sandra	サンドラ
Sarah	サラ
Sofia/Sophia/Sofie	ソフィア
Steven/Steve	スティーブン・スティーブ
Susan	スーザン
Thomas/Tom	トーマス・トム
Victor/Viktor	ビクター
William/Will/Bill	ウィリアム・ウィル・ビル

List of hiragana & katakana
ひらがな・カタカナ一覧 表

Basic characters 清音

あ ア a	い イ i	う ウ u	え エ e	お オ o
か カ ka	き キ ki	く ク ku	け ケ ke	こ コ ko
さ サ sa	し シ shi	す ス su	せ セ se	そ ソ so
た タ ta	ち チ chi	つ ツ tsu	て テ te	と ト to
な ナ na	に ニ ni	ぬ ヌ nu	ね ネ ne	の ノ no
は ハ ha	ひ ヒ hi	ふ フ fu	へ ヘ he	ほ ホ ho
ま マ ma	み ミ mi	む ム mu	め メ me	も モ mo
や ヤ ya		ゆ ユ yu		よ ヨ yo
ら ラ ra	り リ ri	る ル ru	れ レ re	ろ ロ ro
わ ワ wa				を ヲ o
ん ン n				

Voiced consonants & Semi-voiced consonants
濁音・半濁音
<ruby>濁音<rt>だくおん</rt></ruby>・<ruby>半濁音<rt>はんだくおん</rt></ruby>

が ガ ga	ぎ ギ gi	ぐ グ gu	げ ゲ ge	ご ゴ go
ざ ザ za	じ ジ ji	ず ズ zu	ぜ ゼ ze	ぞ ゾ zo
だ ダ da	ぢ ヂ ji	づ ヅ zu	で デ de	ど ド do
ば バ ba	び ビ bi	ぶ ブ bu	べ ベ be	ぼ ボ bo
ぱ パ pa	ぴ ピ pi	ぷ プ pu	ぺ ペ pe	ぽ ポ po

Contracted sounds 拗音

きゃ キャ kya	きゅ キュ kyu	きょ キョ kyo
しゃ シャ sha	しゅ シュ shu	しょ ショ sho
ちゃ チャ cha	ちゅ チュ chu	ちょ チョ cho
にゃ ニャ nya	にゅ ニュ nyu	にょ ニョ nyo
ひゃ ヒャ hya	ひゅ ヒュ hyu	ひょ ヒョ hyo
みゃ ミャ mya	みゅ ミュ myu	みょ ミョ myo
りゃ リャ rya	りゅ リュ ryu	りょ リョ ryo

Contracted sounds(Voiced consonants & Semi-voiced consonants)　拗音の濁音・半濁音

ぎゃ ギャ gya	ぎゅ ギュ gyu	ぎょ ギョ gyo
じゃ ジャ ja	じゅ ジュ ju	じょ ジョ jo
びゃ ビャ bya	びゅ ビュ byu	びょ ビョ byo
ぴゃ ピャ pya	ぴゅ ピュ pyu	ぴょ ピョ pyo

Index

●著者紹介

Bret Mayer　ブレット・メイヤー

アメリカ・ニュージャージー州出身。高校生の頃、『ドラゴンボール』をはじめ、漫画やアニメがきっかけで漢字が生き甲斐となる。2012年に非漢字文化圏出身者として初めて日本漢字能力検定1級に合格。

Born in New Jersey, USA, Bret Mayer was first captivated by kanji in high school thanks to *Dragon Ball* among other manga/anime. In 2012, Mayer became the first westerner to pass grade 1 of the Japan Kanji Aptitude Test.

カバーデザイン	斉藤 啓（ブッダプロダクションズ）
本文デザイン/DTP	株式会社　センターメディア
イラスト	イクタケ マコト/バラマツ ヒトミ/Bret Mayer
筆文字	竹内 一
ダウンロード音声制作	一般財団法人　英語教育協議会（ELEC）
ナレーター	水月優希

本書へのご意見・ご感想は下記URLまでお寄せください。
http://www.jresearch.co.jp/contact/

はじめてのひらがな・カタカナ
Let's Explore HIRAGANA & KATAKANA

平成30年（2018年）7月10日　初版第1刷発行

著　者	Bret Mayer
発行人	福田富与
発行所	有限会社　Jリサーチ出版
	〒166-0002 東京都杉並区高円寺北2-29-14-705
	電話03（6808）8801（代）　FAX 03（5364）5310
	編集部03（6808）8806
	http://www.jresearch.co.jp
印刷所	（株）シナノ　パブリッシングプレス

ISBN 978-4-86392-394-2　禁無断転載。なお、乱丁・落丁はお取り替えいたします。

How to Download Audio Files

STEP1

Visit https://audiobook.jp/exchange/jresearch
* ※ Enter the above URL into your preferred browser or visit the publisher's official site (http://www.jresearch.co.jp) and click the banner labelled 「音声ダウンロード」.

STEP2

Complete registration for a free membership at audiobook.jp.
* ※ Download of the audio files requires completion of (free!) member registration at audiobook.jp. Click 「無料会員登録」 to begin. Enter your name 「名前」, email 「メールアドレス」 and desired password 「パスワード」.

STEP3

After registration, return to https://audiobook.jp/exchange/jresearch . Enter your serial number in the input box labeled 「シリアルコード入力欄」 and click the turquoise button labeled 「送信する」 below.
* ※ The files will now be added to your Library 「ライブラリ」.

STEP4

Download your desired audio files!
* ※ If using a smartphone, instruction will appear for downloading the 「audiobook.jp」 app. You can also find the app by searching "otobank inc." or 「オーディオブック」 in the iOS or Android app store.
* ※ If using a PC, click 「ライブラリ」 from the left-side menu and select your desired files.

[! NOTE !]

* You can play the audio files on PC or iPhone/Android smartphones and tablets.
* There is no limit to how many times you can download and play the files.
* For help regarding download of the audio files, please e-mail info@febe.jp (weekdays between 10AM-8PM, Japanese only)